47 Easy-to-Do Classic Science Experiments

by
EUGENE F. PROVENZO, JR.
and
ASTERIE BAKER PROVENZO

Illustrations Prepared by PETER A. ZORN, JR.

DOVER PUBLICATIONS, INC., NEW YORK

To the memory of
Charles D. Baker
and
Edward Barnes

Copyright © 1989 by Eugene F. Provenzo, Jr.,
Asterie Baker Provenzo, and Peter A. Zorn, Jr.
All rights reserved under Pan American and
International Copyright Conventions.

Published in Canada by General Publishing Company, Ltd.,
30 Lesmill Road, Don Mills, Toronto, Ontario.
Published in the United Kingdom by Constable and Company, Ltd.,
10 Orange Street, London WC2H 7EG.

47 Easy-to-Do Classic Science Experiments is a new work,
first published by Dover Publications, Inc., in 1989.

Manufactured in the United States of America
Dover Publications, Inc.
31 East 2nd Street
Mineola, N.Y. 11501

Library of Congress Cataloging-in-Publication Data

Provenzo, Eugene F.
    47 easy-to-do classic science experiments / by Eugene F. Provenzo, Jr.,
and Asterie Baker Provenzo ; illustrations prepared by Peter A. Zorn, Jr.
        p.   cm.
    Summary: Forty-seven popular science experiments of the past, all of
which can be performed with household materials, and dealing with such
principles as air pressure, buoyancy, gravity, inertia, and sound.
    ISBN 0-486-25856-4
    1. Science—Experiments—Juvenile literature. [1. Science—Experi-
ments. 2. Experiments.] I. Provenzo, Asterie Baker. II. Zorn, Peter A., ill.
III. Title. IV. Title: Forty-seven easy-to-do classic science experiments.
Q164.P88   1989
507′.8—dc19   88-31334
                                                                    CIP
                                                                    AC

Table of Contents

Introduction

47 Easy-to-Do Classic Science Experiments is a book intended to help you rediscover the magic of some of the most popular science experiments of the past. The book includes 47 simple, but fun, science experiments that don't require any special or costly equipment and can be conducted easily at home or school. Many of these experiments have been known for hundreds, even thousands of years!

Nearly all of the experiments included in this book can be done with simple materials found in most households. Tissue paper, scissors, tapes, rubber balloons, pens and pencils are typical of the types of materials required.

Underlying the development of this book is the assumption that we learn best by discovering things for ourselves. Each experiment includes a historical illustration of the experiment being conducted, a description of the experiment that often includes an explanation of its history, a list of materials needed to conduct the experiment, the definition of key terms related to the experiment, an explanation of what will be discovered and finally a description, frequently with simple drawings, of how to do the experiment yourself.

A short book like this cannot introduce all of the principles of science. Instead, it is intended to serve as a sampler of some of the best simple science experiments from the past. For those interested in using the experiments to demonstrate specific scientific principles or to supplement a science curriculum unit, we have included a chart, immediately following this Introduction, that classifies each of the experiments. Experiments demonstrating similar principles are grouped together in the text. When used in a classroom setting, the experiments can be copied and handed out individually to the students, used in groups, or used by the entire class together.

In putting this book together, we have drawn upon many nineteenth- and early twentieth-century books and magazines dealing with popular science. The sources of all of the historical illustrations are listed at the end of the book.

NOTE: Many of the definitions used in this book are adapted from E. L. Thorndike and Clarence L. Barnhart, *Scott, Foresman Intermediate Dictionary,* Doubleday Edition (Garden City, New York: Doubleday & Company, Inc., 1979).

Classification Chart of Experiments

The experiments in this book are organized according to the scientific principles they demonstrate. Many of them, however, demonstrate more than one principle. This classification chart will serve as a kind of subject index to such experiments. If an experiment appears under more than one heading, its title is printed in all capital (uppercase) letters only when listed under the primary principle it demonstrates; titles listed only under a single principle are also given in all capital letters. In all instances where you find an experiment title in all capital letters, the name of the principle under which it is listed is identical with the title of the chapter in which the experiment appears. When an experiment is listed under a principle of secondary importance (with respect to that experiment), its title is given in small (lowercase) letters (except for necessary capitals).

Air Pressure
AIR "BOILS" WATER
AIR HOLDS UP WATER
MAGDEBURG SPHERE
SIMPLE DIVING BELL
CARTESIAN DIVER
SOAP-BUBBLE PASSENGER
SUSPENDED PEA
BLOWING AN EGG OUT OF
   A CUP
AIR GLUE

Binocular Vision
3-D vision

Buoyancy
Cartesian diver

Center of Gravity
uphill-rolling object
acrobatic coin
domino acrobatics

Centrifugal Force
water that won't spill
elevated napkin ring
spinning marble

Chemical Absorption
MOISTURE-DETECTING
   MERMAID

Color
color tops
Newton's rings

Density
mixing a liquid parfait

Elasticity
how many quarters will a glass full
   of water hold?
floating needle
snuffing a candle with a soap bubble
soap-bubble passenger

1.
Surface Tension

How Many Quarters Will a Glass Full of Water Hold?

Science makes it possible to perform some wonderful tricks on your friends. For example, suppose you fill a glass with water right to the top. Then ask a friend how many quarters they think you can drop into the glass without causing the water to overflow. No doubt, they will say one or two. The fact is, as the illustration below shows, the answer is more like ten!

How to Drop Quarters Into a Full Glass of Water Without Causing It to Overflow

MATERIALS   ten to twelve quarters
glass full of water

KEY TERMS   Surface tension: The property of a liquid (possessed by all liquids) that causes its surface to contract and resemble a thin, invisible elastic skin.

Convex: Curved outward.

WHAT WILL BE   The surface tension of the water allows the surface
DISCOVERED   to stretch to a high, convex shape before it breaks and the water overflows.

Be sure that the glass is filled with water to the very rim. The surface of the water should be slightly convex.

Carefully, with a steady hand, drop one quarter into the water. Add another and another to the water. As the coins are dropped into the water, you will be able to see that the surface of the water is becoming more and more convex owing to the principles of gravity and surface tension. It will be astonishing how many quarters can be dropped into the glass and how convex the surface of the water will become before the water overflows.

Floating Needle

Two variations of a very simple experiment in surface tension are illustrated below. In both experiments, a needle is made to float on the surface of water in a glass.

How to Float a Needle on Water

MATERIALS   fork
sewing needle
glass full of water

KEY TERMS   Surface tension: The property of a liquid (possessed by all liquids) that causes its surface to contract and resemble a thin, invisible elastic skin.

Even though the needle is heavier than the amount of water it displaces and should sink, it will float because of an invisible elastic skin on the surface of the water. When water comes into contact with air, the molecules on the surface of the water bond together to form a thin, elastic film over the surface.

Place the sewing needle on the fork and gently let the fork down into the glass filled with water. If you are careful, you can remove the fork, and the needle will remain floating on the surface of the water. This trick is possible because the surface of the needle that isn't touching the water remains dry.

The experiment will be even more successful if you oil the needle by rubbing it between your fingers. But remember, the needle must remain dry or it will sink.

In the second version of the experiment, a piece of tissue paper is placed on the surface of the water in the glass. The needle is carefully placed on the tissue paper. As the paper becomes soaked with water, it will sink to the bottom of the glass, leaving the needle floating on the surface of the water.

Snuffing a Candle with a Soap Bubble

The elasticity of a soap bubble is very much like that of a balloon. Both a balloon and a soap bubble can be greatly expanded by having air forced into them. As the experiment illustrated below demonstrates, the surface tension of a soap bubble can exert a force that is actually strong enough to snuff a candle.

How to Snuff a Candle with a Soap Bubble

MATERIALS
candle
matches
funnel or bubble blower
detergent or soap-bubble solution

KEY TERMS
Surface tension: The property of a liquid (possessed by all liquids) that causes its surface to contract and resemble a thin, invisible elastic skin.

Elasticity: Elastic quality. Ability of an object to spring back to its original shape after being stretched or squeezed.

The surface tension of the soap bubble causes the
force of the air escaping from the bubble to be
strong enough to snuff the candle.

Light the candle. Coat the mouth of the funnel with detergent or
soap-bubble solution. With a little bit of practice, you should be able
to blow a bubble with a diameter of 12 inches.

Once you can blow a good-sized bubble, place your finger over the
tip of the funnel just after you have blown a large bubble and before
it escapes the funnel. This will prevent the air from escaping.

Place the tip of the funnel next to the candle flame. When you
release your finger, the force of the air escaping will be strong
enough to blow out the candle flame.

Motorized Paper Fish

One of the most interesting devices to appear in magic and science
books during the late 1800's was the paper fish. The books claimed
that a drop of oil could transform a simple piece of paper in the
shape of a fish into a motorized fish that would shoot across the
surface of a bowl of water.

The illustration below shows the pattern for the paper fish that
will swim around the surface of a bowl of water without being
pushed or blown upon.

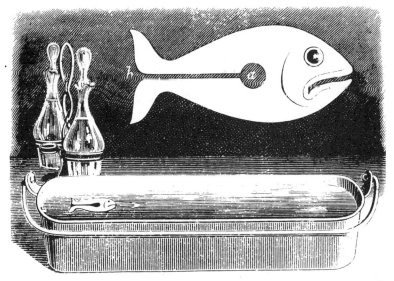

How to Motorize a Paper Fish

MATERIALS   piece of paper
scissors
some vegetable oil or liquid detergent (the type used to wash dishes)
large bowl or loaf cake pan full of water

KEY TERMS   Surface tension: The property of a liquid (possessed by all liquids) that causes its surface to contract and resemble a thin, invisible elastic skin.

WHAT WILL BE DISCOVERED   The lower surface tension of the detergent or oil will push it through the slit in the fish. The flow of detergent or oil will be powerful enough to propel the fish across the water.

Trace the pattern of the fish outlined below onto a piece of paper and cut it out.

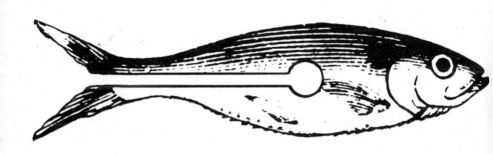

MOTORIZED PAPER FISH PATTERN

Carefully place the paper fish on the surface of the water in the bowl. Place a drop of oil or detergent in the hole in the center of the fish. The detergent or oil will lower the surface tension of the water in this hole.

In a few seconds, the fish will begin to move across the water, propelled by the oil or detergent. The oil or detergent will slowly begin to spread out across the surface of the water in a thin film. Its flow is powerful enough to act as a jet and propel the fish across the water without its being touched or pushed. The fish will continue swimming until the detergent or oil reduces the surface tension of all the water in the bowl.

Perpetual Dancers

There have been many attempts to build perpetual-motion machines. None of them have been successful. However, there is a simple device that is based on the principle of surface tension that will appear to move almost endlessly.

The device was described in a number of scientific books during the late 1800's. In one version, a piece of camphor (the substance from which mothballs were made) was placed in a small tin boat. A small hole was cut at the back of the boat and the camphor was set on top of it. When it came in contact with the water the camphor gradually escaped and spread itself out along the surface of the water. In doing so, it propelled the boat the same way the paper fish is propelled in the previous experiment in this book. A device of the type described can run for a remarkably long time. In fact, a special version of the device in the form of a dancing couple might run for several days without stopping.

How to Make a Set of Perpetual Dancers

MATERIALS
four needles
1″ × 1″ cork (or two 1″ × ½″-thick corks)
X-Acto knife (or similar sharp implement)
several mothballs (no longer made of camphor, but still effective)
model-airplane glue

KEY TERMS
Surface tension: The property of a liquid (possessed by all liquids) that causes its surface to contract and resemble a thin, invisible elastic skin.

WHAT WILL BE DISCOVERED
The lowered surface tension of the water in which the "camphor" dissolves will push the "camphor" along the surface of the water. The flow of the "camphor" will be powerful enough to propel the device around and around.

Carefully cut the cork so that you have two disks approximately 1 inch in diameter and ½ inch thick. Cut one disk like a pie, into four slices ½ inch by ½ inch. Stick the four needles into the remaining disk of cork to form a cross. On the end of each needle fit a small piece of cork with a piece of mothball glued to it as illustrated below. Be sure that you glue the "camphor" onto the cork and attach the pieces of cork to the needles exactly as shown below.

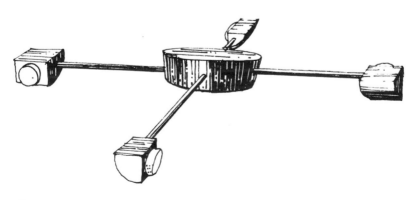

If you like, you can photocopy or otherwise copy the pattern below for a pair of dancing figures. Cut out the pair and glue the tab to the top of the center cork. When set in the water, the device will continue spinning on the surface of the water for several days.

PERPETUAL DANCERS PATTERN

2.
Air Pressure

Air "Boils" Water

We live at the bottom of an ocean of air. This air, which is essential to all forms of life, is really a mixture of gases. Just as solids and liquids are affected by the forces of gravity, so are the gases in the air. They occupy space; they have weight. The pressure caused by the weight of air can help you perform some amazing scientific magic tricks.

For example, the illustration below shows a demonstration of air pressure in which an upside-down glass of water doesn't spill through the handkerchief covering it! Then, for a second trick, it is possible to cause the water inside the glass to bubble as though it were boiling without being heated.

How to Make Water Bubble Without Heating It

MATERIALS
large handkerchief
small glass
water

KEY TERMS
Air pressure: Pressure caused by the weight of the air at the top of the atmosphere as it presses down upon the air beneath it.

Surface tension: The property of a liquid (possessed by all liquids) that causes its surface to contract and resemble a thin, invisible elastic skin.

Gas: A substance that is not a liquid or a solid; a substance that has no shape or size of its own and can expand without limit.

Concave: Curved inward.

WHAT WILL BE DISCOVERED
Air pressure will keep the water from spilling out of the upside-down glass. Surface tension will prevent the water from seeping through the handkerchief. When a vacuum is caused to form at the bottom of the glass, air pressure causes air to penetrate the handkerchief and bubble through the water to fill the vacuum.

Fill the glass three-fourths full of water. Cover it with a handkerchief as though you were a magician and were going to make the glass disappear. Pick up the glass with one hand. Pull the handkerchief's edges under the bottom of the glass with the other hand. Hold the base of the glass and the handkerchief with one hand. Then press in on the center of the handkerchief just far enough so that it just barely touches the water (see part 1 of the illustration). Do not worry when the handkerchief becomes wet; this will actually make the trick work better.

Turn the glass upside-down as shown in part 3 of the illustration. No water should penetrate the handkerchief and the concave shape of the handkerchief will be maintained.

Now for your second trick. Hold the glass steady in the same position with one hand. With the other hand, draw the handkerchief tighter so that the concave shape becomes level, like the head of a drum. The water will drop to the new level, but will not spill through the handkerchief. A vacuum is formed at the bottom of the glass, however. Air will penetrate the handkerchief to fill this vacuum. As the air passes through the water it will bubble, as seen in part 2 of the illustration. The water will look and sound as though it is boiling without even being heated!

Air Holds Up Water

Air pressure makes it possible to perform some wonderful tricks with a glass of water. One of the easiest and yet most amazing demonstrations of this principle occurs when a glass of water is turned upside down and the water doesn't spill!

How to Turn a Glass of Water Upside Down
Without Spilling a Drop

MATERIALS   drinking glass
                sheet of paper
                water

KEY TERMS   Air pressure: Pressure caused by the weight of the air at the top of the atmosphere as it presses down upon the air beneath it.

Air has pressure. The water will be prevented from spilling because the pressure of the air outside the glass is greater than the pressure inside the glass.

Fill the glass full of water. Place the sheet of paper over the top of the glass. Hold the piece of paper in place over the top of the glass with one hand. Turn the glass upside down with the other hand.

As you move the glass closer to the surface of a table, desk or countertop, remove your hand from the piece of paper, and place the glass on the table. Then, carefully lift the glass just enough to quickly slip the piece of paper out from under the glass. Air pressure will hold the water in the glass even as you lift it slightly to remove the piece of paper.

It is easy to make this demonstration even more dramatic. Fill one glass of water and set it on the table right-side-up. Fill a second glass of water. Cover the second glass of water with a piece of paper and then invert the glass.

Place the second glass on top of the first. Be sure that the rim of the second glass fits exactly on the rim of the first glass. Then lift the second glass just enough to slip out the piece of paper. Again, air pressure will hold the water in the inverted glass, sitting on top of the first glass, without spilling a drop. (When first practising these experiments, however, it is wisest to perform them in or over a sink!)

Magdeburg Sphere

One of the most important experiments in air pressure was performed around 1650 by Otto von Guericke (1602–1686), the mayor of Magdeburg, Germany, and a scientist. He placed two giant, hollow metal half-spheres together. Then he removed almost all the air from the inside of the combined hemispheres with a crude vacuum pump that he had invented himself. A team of horses was attached to the end of each hemisphere, and the teams were driven in opposite directions. No matter how hard the horses pulled, they could not pull the two hemispheres apart.

In von Guericke's experiment, the air pressure on the outside of the combined metal spheres was much greater than on the interior. In fact, it was so great that it was able to hold the two half-spheres together even when the teams of horses were trying to pull them apart.

As you can see in the illustration (from an 1887 *Scientific American Supplement*), the principle of the Magdeburg sphere can be demonstrated much more simply.

How to Demonstrate the Principle of the Magdeburg Sphere

MATERIALS
short candle
heavy piece of paper
two drinking glasses of the same size
water
matches
scissors

KEY TERMS
Air pressure: Pressure caused by the weight of the air at the top of the atmosphere as it presses down upon the air beneath it.

Vacuum pump: A pump used to remove air from an enclosure.

Suction: The process of drawing a liquid or gas from a space by sucking out or removing part of it to produce a vacuum.

Hemisphere: half of a sphere or globe.

WHAT WILL BE
DISCOVERED
The burning candle will reduce the air pressure in the bottom glass. Some air in the top glass will seep through the porous paper to the lower glass and the vacuum will be distributed through both glasses, making it impossible to pull the glasses apart.

Cut the paper so that it overlaps the top of either glass by about one-half inch all around. Place the piece of paper on the open top of the first glass. Dampen the paper thoroughly.

Set the candle inside the second glass, resting it on the bottom of the glass. Light the candle.

Now, carefully place the first glass (with the piece of dampened paper over its top) upside-down on top of the second glass with the lit candle in it. Make sure you fit the mouths of the glasses together perfectly.

The candle will fade out almost immediately because it quickly uses up all of the oxygen inside the glass. In doing so, it will have reduced the atmospheric pressure in the lower glass just as von Guericke used the vacuum pump to reduce the pressure inside his hemispheres. Some of the air from the top glass passes through the porous paper, distributing the vacuum. The damp paper seals the edges.

Try to lift the top glass off the lower one. You will find that you probably can't pull them apart because the air pressure outside the glasses is now more powerful. Now you know how suction, which actually results from the difference in air pressures, works.

NOTE: In order to separate the glasses, twist them apart instead of trying to pull them apart. This will break the vacuum.

Simple Diving Bell

The first device which enabled people to breathe under water was the diving bell. Diving bells have been used for hundreds of years. In fact, legend has it that in the fourth century B.C., Alexander the Great descended in a diving bell into the waters off the coast of what is now Turkey.

Bell-shaped diving hulls are open to the water at the bottom. Air from the surface is passed into the bell through a hose. As you will see by putting together a very simple diving bell with a glass and bowl of water, the air pressure within the bell keeps the water from entering it.

How to Make a Simple Diving Bell

MATERIALS
: a deep bowl full of water
a glass
a piece of paper

KEY TERMS
: Air pressure: Pressure caused by the weight of the air at the top of the atmosphere as it presses down upon the air beneath it.

WHAT WILL BE DISCOVERED
: When water is forced into the diving bell (glass) the air inside will be compressed until the air pressure inside the glass equals the pressure of the water. This prevents the water from completely filling up the inside of the glass so that a space in the glass will remain dry. In a full-size diving bell, there remains enough air for a diver to breathe.

Fill the bowl with water. Crumple the piece of paper into a ball and stuff it into the top of the glass. Place the glass upside-down in the bowl. Be careful not to tilt the glass.

The water will rise slightly into the glass, but not enough to wet the paper. What has happened is that as the water enters the glass it has compressed the air inside. When squeezed into a smaller space the pressure of the air in the glass increases, preventing the water from completely filling the glass. As you can see, the interior of the glass is like a simple diving bell. The bottom of a diving bell would be open, just like the glass, so that the divers could enter and leave the chamber.

Cartesian Diver

The Cartesian diver was invented in the early 1600's by the French mathematician and philosopher René Descartes (1596–1650). The device was made from a tall glass vessel or bottle.

When the bottle was filled almost to the top with water, a small glass figure of a man was placed in the water. A piece of rubber was then stretched across the top of the bottle. When pressure was applied to the top of the piece of rubber, the figure would descend. When the pressure on the rubber covering was released, the figure would rise up through the water.

How to Make a Cartesian Diver

MATERIALS
tall, widemouthed glass jar, filled almost to the top
    with water
balloon
one small, empty plastic medicine bottle
cellophane, or similar adhesive, tape
large metal washer
X-Acto knife (or similar cutting implement)

KEY TERMS
Cartesian: Of or pertaining to the methods or
philosophy of the mathematician and philosopher
Descartes.

Air pressure: Pressure caused by the weight of the
air at the top of the atmosphere as it presses down
upon the air beneath it.

Buoyancy: Ability to float.

WHAT WILL BE
DISCOVERED
When you press your hand against the water, the
air pressure inside the jar changes. However, since,

18

for all practical purposes, water can't be compressed, it will be forced to rise up into the diver (the small bottle). The diver will become heavier, lose some of its buoyancy and begin to sink. When you remove your hand the bottle will rise again.

Tape the large metal washer to the top of the plastic medicine bottle to weight it as illustrated below. Cut out the tape directly above the hole in the washer.

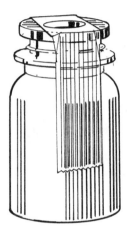

Push the small medicine bottle with the washer upside-down into the glass jar, tilting it so that water flows into the bottle and just enough air remains in it to keep it barely afloat. The bottom of the medicine bottle should come just barely to the surface of the water.

Stretch the balloon across the mouth of the jar and hold it tight with one hand. Now press down on the top of the balloon with your other hand. The bottle, or diver, should descend because, by pressing down on the balloon, you change the air pressure inside the bottle. The pressure you exert on the balloon forces the water into the bottle. This in turn pushes the air into a smaller space, compressing it. As the bottle fills up with water, it becomes heavier, losing some of its buoyancy and beginning to sink.

When you release the pressure you have applied to the balloon, the pressure will likewise be released from the water. The lighter air will then expand and force some water to flow out of the bottle. As the bottle becomes lighter it will again buoy or float up.

NOTE: This is a tricky experiment to do. It may take some experimenting to get just the right amount of water into the plastic medicine bottle so that it will neither sink nor be too buoyant.

Soap-Bubble Passenger

With a little bit of patience and practice it is possible to get a soap bubble to carry a payload. In the case of the demonstration illustrated below, the payload attached to the soap bubble is a paper man.

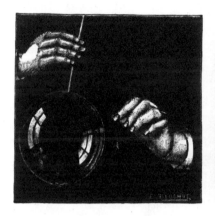 

How to Attach a Paper Man to a Soap Bubble

MATERIALS	tissue paper
	pencil
	scissors
	lightweight thread
	ruler
	soap-bubble solution
	blow tube or bubble pipe
KEY TERMS	Film: A very thin sheet, surface or coating, often of a liquid.
	Surface: The outside of anything.
	Air pressure: Pressure caused by the weight of the air at the top of the atmosphere as it presses down upon the air beneath it.
WHAT WILL BE DISCOVERED	The hot air blown into the soap bubble from your lungs will cause the bubble to rise. The surface film of the soap bubble can support an attached object without bursting.

Trace the pattern of the man and the small disk illustrated below onto the piece of tissue paper. Cut out the two pieces. Cut a two- or three-inch piece of thread. Punch a small hole in the center of the disk and in the loop on the umbrella over the man's head. Thread opposite ends of the piece of thread through these two holes and secure the ends by tying knots. The man and the disk should now be connected by the piece of thread.

Blow a large bubble. While the bubble is still connected to the bubble pipe or blow tube, gently attach the small paper disk to the surface of the bubble by simple contact with the bubble as shown in the first illustration above.

Gently release the soap bubble from the bubble pipe or blow tube with a flick of your wrist. The hot air you have blown from your lungs into the bubble will cause it to rise like a hot-air balloon. The paper man will slide to the lower side of the bubble and remain suspended as it rises.

If the temperature of the air surrounding the bubble is cool, it will probably burst when it hits the ceiling. If the room temperature is hot, the bubble will slowly descend as it cools off.

SOAP-BUBBLE PASSENGER PATTERN

Suspended Pea

It is possible to use a characteristic of a jet of air to help you perform some scientific magic. As illustrated below, you can use a jet of air from a pipe to hold a pea in place. And if the pea has a pin stuck through it, it will even revolve in place.

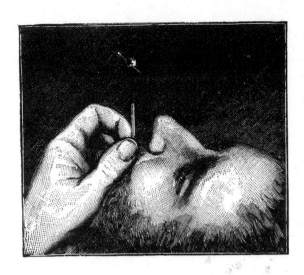

How to Demonstrate the Attraction of a Jet of Air

MATERIALS

pea, or small spherical object
straight pin
soda straw
scissors

KEY TERMS

Jet: Stream of air, water, steam or any liquid or gas, sent with force, especially from a small opening.

Air pressure: Pressure caused by the weight of the air at the top of the atmosphere as it presses down upon the air beneath it.

WHAT WILL BE DISCOVERED

Because, like all moving gases, the air in the jet stream is at a lower pressure than the still air around it, the surrounding air will push the pea back in position when it tries to escape.

If the pea is dry, soak it in water to soften it so that you can push the pin through its center without splitting it. Push the straight pin through the center of the pea. Cut a two-inch piece from the soda straw. Place the pea on one end of the piece of soda straw in such a way that one of the ends of the pin sticks down into the straw and holds the pea in place.

Tilt your head back in a horizontal position. Put the other end of the soda straw in your mouth as shown in the illustration. Gently blow through the straw. The jet of air will lift the pea. As you blow with more force, the pea will rise higher, and, if you maintain a regular jet of air, it will remain suspended in the same position. As the ends of the pin receive thrusts from the jet of air, the pea will also revolve.

Blowing an Egg Out of a Cup

If a bullet is shot from a gun through a glass window, it passes through the glass, leaving a neat round hole. However, if the bullet is thrown against the same window pane, it shatters the glass into fragments. In the first case, the bullet is shot with such force that it passes through the window too rapidly for the pane as a whole to react. In the second case, the bullet naturally cannot be thrown with such extreme force, and therefore the window glass shatters as if it had been hit by a thrown rock.

Another example of this principle is illustrated below. The power of air put into rapid motion can create such pressure as to cause an egg to jump out of a cup.

How to Make an Egg Jump Out of a Cup by
Blowing on It

MATERIALS   hard-boiled egg
one or two short coffee cups

KEY TERMS   Air pressure: Pressure caused by the weight of the
air at the top of the atmosphere as it presses down
upon the air beneath it.

WHAT WILL BE   Air, put in rapid motion, has the power, as does
DISCOVERED   atmospheric pressure, to lift an object, such as an
egg, out of a cup.

Place the hard-boiled egg in one cup. Blow vigorously into it. With
a little practice and good lungs, you should be able to get the egg to
jump out of the cup. You might even be able to get it to land in the
second cup!

Air Glue

Air pressure is responsible for many "scientific tricks," such as the
one illustrated below. You can make a quarter stick to wood without
using glue, tape or any other adhesive.

How to Stick a Quarter to Wood
with Air

MATERIALS
: quarter
wood side of a piece of furniture or a door

KEY TERMS
: Air pressure: Pressure caused by the weight of the air at the top of the atmosphere as it presses down upon the air beneath it.

Vacuum: An empty space without air in it.

WHAT WILL BE DISCOVERED
: When the quarter is rubbed against the wood, the air between the quarter and the wood is eliminated, creating a vacuum. Therefore, the pressure surrounding the quarter is strong enough to hold it against the wood.

Place a quarter flat against a vertical side of a piece of unpainted wood furniture or a door. For this trick to work, the piece of furniture or door must be heavily waxed with beeswax or a natural wax. Rub the coin briskly, up and down, pressing it firmly against the wood as you rub.

After a few minutes of rubbing, remove your hand and you will discover that the quarter sticks to the wood. Because of the pressure and friction created by rubbing the quarter against the wood, the thin layer of air between the wood and the coin was heated, expanded and partially expelled. When you stop moving the coin back and forth, it cools quickly, causing a lower air pressure between the coin and the wood. The pressure of the air surrounding the quarter is then sufficient to hold it in place against the wood.

3.
Optics

3-D Vision

For over two thousand years, scientists have known that each of our eyes sees a different image when we look at something. Each eye transmits what it sees to the brain where the two different images are combined to give us a unified, three-dimensional view of the world around us. The image that is created is known as a "binocular image."

Illustrated below, from a nineteenth-century book on science, is an intriguing optical illusion that demonstrates the principle of binocular vision.

How to Demonstrate Binocular Vision

MATERIALS   one 3″ × 5″ index or other paper card

KEY TERMS   Binocular: Using both eyes at once.

WHAT WILL BE   Your brain combines the two different images it
DISCOVERED   receives from each eye into a single picture.

In order to see how binocular vision works you will need to place the 3 × 5 index card along the dotted line on the pattern below, at a right angle to the page, just as the man in the previous illustration is doing.

Lower your nose toward the card until it touches the card. As you do so, you will see the bird fly backward into the cage. This will happen because your brain is combining the two different images it is receiving from your eyes into a single picture, or a binocular image.

Thaumatrope

In 1826 the English physician J. A. Paris invented the thaumatrope, or "wonder turner." The thaumatrope consists of a piece of cardboard with a picture drawn on each side, the two pictures being upside-down relative to each other. Two pieces of string are attached to the cardboard and are used to spin it. When the thaumatrope is rapidly spun, the two different pictures merge into one, providing the illusion of a single picture. The thaumatrope is believed to be the first cinematographic device.

How to Make a Thaumatrope

MATERIALS
: 3″-square piece of cardboard
pencil or felt-tip pen
scissors
two 6″ pieces of string

KEY TERMS
: Cinematograph: Motion-picture camera, viewer or show. Motion pictures are actually a connected series of pictures projected on a screen or seen in a

THAUMATROPE PATTERNS

viewer in such rapid succession that the spectator gets the impression that the people and objects pictured are moving.

WHAT WILL BE DISCOVERED When an image is projected onto the retina of your eye it remains there, unchanged, for one-tenth to one-twentieth of a second. This is the principle of the persistence of vision, which makes it possible for two different images to merge into one.

Cut a circle three inches in diameter out of the cardboard. Near the edges of the circle, punch two holes 180 degrees apart from each other (exactly opposite each other). Attach a piece of string through each hole.

Photocopy or trace the patterns for the two pictures. Glue one onto each side of the cardboard. Be sure that the drawings are directly opposite each other and upside-down relative to each other.

Hold the string between your fingers and twist it to spin the thaumatrope. The two pictures should merge into one because of the principle of the persistence of vision.

Moving-Picture Machine

The stroboscope is a device that was invented in 1832 by the Belgian physicist J. A. F. Plateau. It is a simple device that allows motion to be slowed so that a moving object appears either slower than it actually is or stationary. The phantascope is a variation of the stroboscope and makes it possible to observe sequential pictures as though they are actually moving.

The discovery of the phantascope is often credited to the Austrian geologist S. von Stampfer. It is considered by many people to be the first "moving-picture" device. Below is an illustration of a phantascope disk that appeared in the November 26, 1881, issue of *Scientific American*.

How to Make a Stroboscope/Phantascope

MATERIALS   piece of lightweight cardboard
                          scissors
                          thumbtack

unsharpened pencil
mirror
X-Acto knife (or similar cutting tool)

KEY TERMS	Sequential: Forming a sequence or connected series.
WHAT WILL BE DISCOVERED	When an image is projected onto the retina of your eye it remains there, unchanged, for one-tenth to one-twentieth of a second. This is the principle of the persistence of vision, which makes it possible for two different images to merge into one, creating the illusion that the horse on the phantascope disk is actually running.

Make a copy of the pattern illustrated below. Glue it onto the piece of cardboard and cut it out. Cut out the viewing slits in the center of the device with the X-Acto knife. Attach the disk to the end of the pencil with the thumbtack as illustrated. Make sure that the side illustrated with the horses faces away from the side that the pencil is on.

31

In order to use the device you have made as a stroboscope, rotate the disk and look through the slits at a moving object such as a fan that is turned on or the pendulum of a clock. By experimenting with the speed at which you spin the disk, you will be able to slow down the motion of the object.

In order to make your stroboscope work as a phantascope, stand in front of a mirror and rotate it quickly, looking through the slits. Make sure that you focus on one of the images of the horses reflected in the mirror. Experiment with different speeds. Do not spin the phantascope too fast. You should be able to see the horses move!

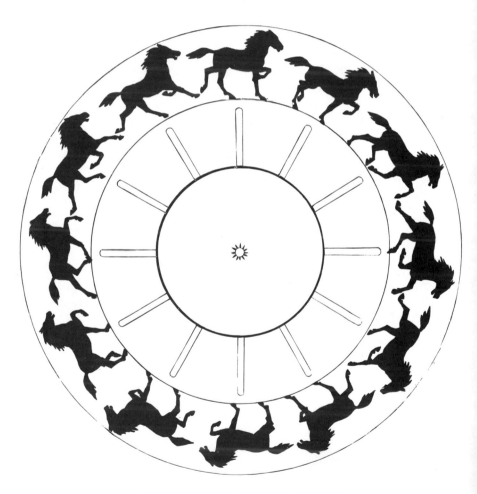

STROBOSCOPE/PHANTASCOPE PATTERN

Distorted Picture

The oldest known example of an anamorphosis can be found in the notebooks of the great Italian inventor and artist Leonardo da Vinci (1452–1519). The word "anamorphosis" is derived from a Greek word meaning "to transform." The technique has been used since the discovery of perspective drawing in the 1400's to conceal political messages in paintings, or simply to create amusing pictures like the English anamorphosis from the mid-1800's illustrated below.

How to View an Anamorphosis

MATERIALS the anamorphosis illustrated above

KEY TERMS Anamorphosis: An image that appears to be distorted and unrecognizable except when viewed from a special angle or reflected in a curved mirror; then the distortion disappears and the image appears normal.

Perspective drawing: The art of drawing pictures of objects on a flat surface so as to give the appearance of distance or depth.

That the principles of perspective drawing make it possible to draw a picture that appears distorted when viewed directly and yet correct when viewed from a special angle.

Hold the anamorphosis in front of you so that the page is perfectly horizontal. Shut one eye. View the picture with the other eye, from a distance of two to three inches from the bottom. You may have to raise, lower or otherwise adjust the position of the picture slightly until the people, the bridge and the buildings appear normal.

Color Tops

During the late 1800's the Scottish physicist James Clerk Maxwell (1831–1879) conducted a number of experiments in which he blended colors using tops. Disks, each of a separate color, were mounted on a spindle. The disks were slit on the side so that they could overlap one another. The different colors merged together when the spindle was spun. Maxwell's experiments were important in leading to an understanding of why some people are color-blind. Below is an illustration of Maxwell's color-blending top.

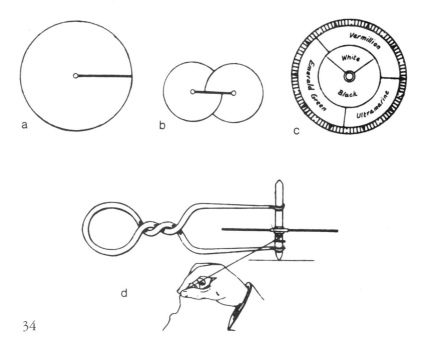

a   b   c

d

34

How to Make a Color Top

four of five sheets of different-colored construction paper
scissors
5″ piece of ¼″ dowel
piece of cardboard
used wooden thread spool
pencil sharpener or penknife
saw
rubber cement or some other type of glue
pair of compasses (for drawing circle)

KEY TERMS

Color: Sensation produced by the effect of waves of light striking the retina of the eye. Different colors are produced by light rays of different wavelengths.

Color-blind: Unable to tell certain colors apart (in extreme cases, unable to perceive any colors).

WHAT WILL BE
DISCOVERED

Separate colors can be blended into a new color because our eyes perceive the mixture of colors only, not the separate colors, when the top is spinning.

Sharpen the end of the piece of doweling in the pencil sharpener or with the penknife. Cut the spool in half with the saw. Force the pointed end of the dowel through half of one of the pieces of spool so that it comes out on the side where you cut it. If the dowel is too loose, wrap a piece of tape around it in order to give you a tight fit. The top should look something like this.

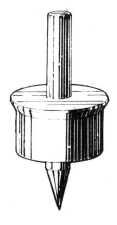

Using the compasses, draw a circle four inches in diameter on the cardboard. Also draw a circle the same size on each different piece of colored paper that you have. Punch or cut a hole in the center of each circle. Cut a slit from the edge to the center of each colored disk. Glue the cardboard circle to the top of the spool. When the glue has dried you can slide the disks on top of the spindle. If you overlap the slits on the colored disks, you will be able to make up different proportions of color. By spinning the top quickly the colors on the disks will combine with one another and blend into a single color.

Newton's Rings

Have you ever noticed the rings of color floating in a patch of oil-covered water in a puddle on the road? The colored rings can also be observed in soap bubbles when light falls on their thin films. These rings of color were first discovered by Sir Isaac Newton (1642–1727), the famous English scientist and mathematician, and have since been known as "Newton's Rings."

Newton discovered that the soap-bubble film acts as a prism. When light passes through a prism, it separates into the full range of different wavelengths that we perceive as the different colors. The water droplets that form a rainbow act in the same way. The colors you see in the soap bubble will vary depending upon its thickness.

How to Demonstrate Newton's Rings
with Soap Bubbles

MATERIALS

detergent or soap-bubble solution
soap-bubble pipe or blower
sugar
small bowl

KEY TERMS

Film: A very thin layer, sheet, surface or coating, often of liquid.

Prism: A transparent solid object, often of glass, having a particular shape, usually with two parallel triangular ends connected by three faces. Prisms can be used to reflect light rays in a specific direction, to refract (i.e., bend) them, and often by refraction to separate a beam of light into its component colors.

Tenuity: Lack of firmness; delicate fragility.

Iridescent: Displaying changing colors; changing colors when moved or turned.

WHAT WILL BE
DISCOVERED

How the film of a soap bubble acts as a prism to create "Newton's Rings" of color.

Mix some sugar into the soap-bubble solution in a bowl. The sugar will make it possible to blow larger bubbles. Blow a soap bubble. At first, while its diameter is still small, the film will be colorless and transparent. However, as you blow more air into the bubble and its diameter increases, the film will become thinner. As the soap bubble increases in tenuity, a brilliant series of rings of color can be seen on its surface. When you release the bubble and it floats through the air its colors will become iridescent.

Distorted Images

Have you ever seen yourself distorted into weird forms and shapes by the concave and convex mirrors at a circus or amusement park? The same optical phenomenon may easily be demonstrated at home or school, as shown below.

How to Create Optical Distortions with Concave and Convex Surfaces

MATERIALS
Any of the following: a large, highly polished spoon; a highly polished silver, brass, aluminum or chrome concave and/or convex surface, such as that of a tea kettle or coffee pot; a silvered light bulb; a Christmas tree ornament; or a brass vase.

KEY TERMS
Concave: Hollowed, curved inward.

Convex: Curved outward.

Distorted: Twisted or pulled out of shape; having its normal appearance altered in shape.

WHAT WILL BE DISCOVERED
How shiny concave and convex surfaces can distort the image of objects placed near them.

Place your hand near the convex side of a spoon, coffee pot or whatever object you have been able to find to use in the demonstration. The convex side of the object will make an excellent convex mirror like those at amusement parks. It will enlarge and distort the image of your hand.

Try finding shiny objects with concave surfaces that you can use to observe a variation of this optical phenomenon. How do concave surfaces distort images of objects?

4.
Static Electricity

Detecting Static Electrical Charges

In 1600 Dr. William Gilbert (1540–1603), an English physician, published a book on his observations and discoveries about magnets. The book also contained a description and illustration of the first electrical instrument in history, known as the "versorium" (which means "thing used for turning").

The versorium, which today is called an electroscope, was used to study the force created between two objects when one is charged with static electricity. It had a light metal needle or pointer that pivoted on top of a pointed rod. When an object, such as a glass rod,

was rubbed with a piece of cloth to charge it with electricity, it was held close to the pointer. The pointer would be attracted to the charged object and turn towards it.

During the late 1800's, simple versoriums such as the one illustrated below were used in experiments to detect the presence of static electrical charges. You can make this simple versorium to use in your own electrical experiments.

How to Make a Versorium

MATERIALS
large cork
needle
sheet of white paper
large, clear glass or jar
piece of silk or wool
pencil
scissors

KEY TERMS
Electroscope: An instrument that can detect the presence of an electrical charge.

Static electricity: The accumulation on an insulated body of electrical charges that do not flow in a current.

Charge: To cause an electrical charge to be formed.

WHAT WILL BE DISCOVERED
How to make and use a versorium to detect the presence of a static electrical charge.

Photocopy or trace the pattern for the needle (detector) onto the piece of paper and cut it out.

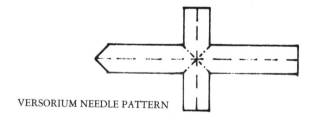

VERSORIUM NEEDLE PATTERN

Crease the paper slightly along the dotted lines. Insert the needle into the cork so that it forms a right angle with the top of the cork. Balance the paper pointer on top of the needle. Place the glass or jar over the pointer and cork as shown in the illustration above.

Vigorously rub the side of the glass with the piece of cloth. The pointer will be attracted to the side of the glass where the static electric charge is being generated. Wherever you move the cloth, the pointer will follow in the same direction.

Electrified Dice

A very simple and popular amusement during the late 1800's was "electrified dice." The dice were cut out of cork. When they were subjected to a static electrical charge, the dice became "electrified" and rolled around.

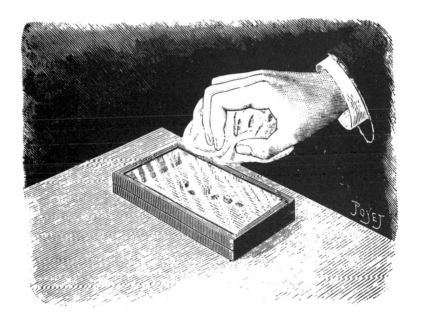

How to Make Electrified Dice

MATERIAL   two cubes of lightweight styrofoam, each the size of a die
felt-tip pen
two large books
small piece of silk or wool
sheet of glass, about 8″ × 10″

KEY TERMS

Electrify: To charge with electricity.

Static electricity: The accumulation on an insulated body of electrical charges that do not flow in a current.

WHAT WILL BE DISCOVERED

The dice will be attracted by the static electrical charge generated by the cloth and will roll around.

Place the piece of glass between the pages of two books so that it is about one inch above the surface of a table.

Mark the cubes of styrofoam with the felt-tip pen so that they look like dice. Place the dice on the table, underneath the glass.

Now quickly rub the piece of silk or wool back and forth over the surface of the glass. Even after you stop rubbing, the dice will continue moving for a while.

NOTE: This experiment is difficult to do in a humid climate.

Dancing Soap Bubbles

Nearly all of us have had the experience of touching a doorhandle after walking across a thick carpet, and receiving a shock. This shock is caused by static electricity, which is generated by the soles of our shoes rubbing against the carpet. As illustrated below, an interesting experiment can be conducted with soap bubbles and static electricity.

How to Make Soap Bubbles Dance

MATERIALS
: one tablespoon sugar
two cups soap-bubble solution
soap-bubble blower or frame
large piece of flannel or wool cloth
piece of paper
clothes brush or hair brush

KEY TERMS
: Static electricity: The accumulation on an insulated body of electrical charges that do not flow in a current.

WHAT WILL BE DISCOVERED
: The piece of paper charged with static electricity will attract the soap bubbles, which are uncharged, lifting them in the air.

Add the sugar to the soap bubble solution. It will make the soap bubbles much stronger and effective for this experiment. Place the piece of flannel or wool over the top of a table or desk.

Gently blow some soap bubbles onto the piece of cloth. Quickly brush the piece of paper vigorously with the brush to generate a static electrical charge.

Hold the piece of paper over some of the soap bubbles. When a bubble is attracted by the charge in the paper it will become elongated, assuming the shape of an egg. As you move the paper closer to the bubble, the magnetic attraction caused by the electrical charge will actually lift the bubble into the air, as though it were dancing or inflated with gas.

43

5.
Magnetism

Floating Magnets

The magnetic swan was a popular toy about a hundred years ago. Basically, it consisted of a wooden swan in which a magnet was imbedded. The swan was then set in the water and a magnet was drawn through the air above it. Depending upon which one of the magnet's poles was closest to the magnetic swan, the swan would move toward or away from the magnet.

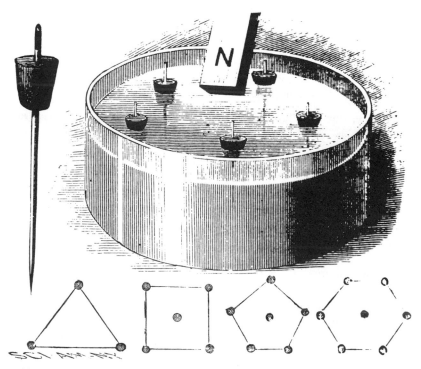

During the 1880's a variation of the toy was developed by the scientist A. M. Mayer to demonstrate some principles of electricity and magnetism. Mayer placed magnetized needles in corks and then set them in water. The needles would form various symmetrical patterns according to the number of needles that were placed in the water.

How to Make Mayer's Floating Needles

MATERIALS	seven small corks seven needles bowl full of water a strong magnet
KEY TERMS	Magnet: A stone or piece of metal that has the property, either natural or induced, of attracting iron. Magnetize: To give the properties or qualities of a magnet to something.
WHAT WILL BE DISCOVERED	The needles will be magnetized with either a north or south polarity (all magnets have poles). Therefore, when you place one pole of the magnet over the bowl it will repel or disperse the needles if it is of the same polarity as the needles. If it is of the opposite polarity, the needles will be drawn together since opposite poles attract each other.

Place the needles together in a bunch. Make sure that they all face the same way. In other words, they eyes of the needles should be next to each other, as should the points of the needles. Magnetize the needles by gently stroking them in one direction with one of the poles of the magnet.

Push the needles through the tops of the corks as shown in the illustration on the previous page. Make sure that only a small part of the eye of the needle is allowed to stick out of the top of the cork.

Set the corks in a bowl of water. By placing one pole of the magnet over the center of the bowl it will be possible to disperse the needles. By using the other pole it will be possible to draw them together. Different numbers of needles set in the water will form different patterns. Examples of these various patterns are shown in the illustration above.

6.
Inertia

Water That Won't Spill

A dramatic demonstration of the principle of centrifugal force is illustrated below. It is actually possible to swing a glass of water around your head without spilling the water. Obviously this is an experiment which requires some practice before attempting to impress others with it!

How to Swing Around a Glass of Water Without Spilling It

MATERIALS   plastic glass or paper cup
                             water

Centrifugal force: The inertia, or tendency to move in one direction, that causes a body turning around a center to move away from the center.

Centrifugal force will hold the water in the glass as the glass is swung around. As you swing the glass, it keeps pushing out in a straight line. The water tends to go straight too, but the glass keeps pushing it toward the center of the circle you are making and forces it to change its direction continually. Thus the water goes in a circular path along with the glass and cannot escape and spill out.

Since the demonstration of centrifugal force is probably going to take a little practice to be successful, it will be a good idea to try it outdoors first.

The first secret of success lies in how you grasp the glass. You must pick it up with your palm facing away from you, as shown below.

The second secret lies in the speed and smoothness with which you swing the glass in a circle. First of all, your arm must be kept straight. Swing the glass in a smooth circle, not too fast or slow. If you jerk your arm the water will probably spill. If you stop the swing abruptly, the water will continue moving in a straight line and slosh all over you. Instead, slow down the swing, coming to a gentle stop, so that the water doesn't spill out of the glass.

47

Magic with Coins

A terrific magic trick that succeeds because of the principle of inertia is illustrated below. It is actually possible to stack one or more coins on your elbow, quickly throw your arm forward and catch the coins in your hand without dropping any on the floor.

How to Perform Magic with Coins

MATERIALS	one or more coins of the same denomination
KEY TERMS	Inertia: The tendency of all objects and matter in the universe to remain still, or, if moving, to go on moving in the same direction unless acted upon by some outside force.
WHAT WILL BE DISCOVERED	It is possible to flip one or more coins off your elbow and catch them in your hand because of the principle of inertia, which keeps the coins from flying off your elbow onto the floor.

Bend your arm as shown in the illustration. Place one or more coins on your elbow. Quickly throw your arm forward and cup your hand. With a little bit of practice you should be able to catch some or even all of the coins in your hand without any falling to the floor. With further practice, you will be able to do this trick with your eyes closed, which will really amaze your friends!

More Magic with Coins

Magic tricks taking advantage of the principle of inertia were very popular during the late 1800's. The experiment illustrated below is from an 1887 *Scientific American Supplement*. It demonstrates that it is actually possible to pile a stack of coins on a plate and then deposit them in the same order on a table by pulling the plate out from under the stack in one swoop.

MATERIALS   eight to ten quarters or nickels (be sure to use all of the same type of coin so that they will stack evenly)
plate
table or desk top

KEY TERMS   Inertia: The tendency of all objects and matter in the universe to remain still, or, if moving, to go on moving in the same direction unless acted upon by some outside force.

WHAT WILL BE   That inertia makes it possible to pull a plate out
DISCOVERED   from under a stack of coins without causing the stack to fall apart.

Evenly stack the coins on the plate. Lift the plate about twelve inches above the table or desk top. Then quickly lower the plate eight inches and pull it toward you. As you pull the plate toward you, the coins will lose their support and will fall to the table in their original position.

Elevated Napkin Ring

Another "scientific trick" from the late 1800's was to lift a napkin ring into the air by making it revolve around a forefinger. As illustrated below, this was a simple experiment, but one that took some practice.

How to Elevate a Napkin Ring

MATERIALS   lightweight napkin ring

KEY TERMS   Centrifugal force: The inertia, or tendency to move in one direction, that causes a body turning around a center to move away from the center.

WHAT WILL BE   Once the napkin ring begins to spin around your
DISCOVERED   finger, centrifugal force will keep pushing it away from your finger at the center and its inertia will keep it moving in the circle, overcoming the force of gravity, even as you raise your finger.

Place one of your forefingers vertically in the middle of a napkin ring lying on a table. Twirl the ring around as rapidly as possible. This experiment requires a quick hand and will probably take some practice.

The action of centrifugal force and the resistance of the ring as it spins around your finger should soon enable you to lift the ring and keep it rotating by simply lifting your hand straight up off the table, without altering the angle of your finger. You might even be able to lift the ring high enough to drop it over the neck of a bottle.

Magic with Checkers

Would you believe that if you shot a candle from a gun it could bore a hole into a pine board a short distance from the gun? This is possible because when the velocity of any body, even a soft candle, is great enough, it may indent another, much harder body upon contact. One aspect of inertia is the tendency of all objects, if moving, to go on moving in the same direction; this explains the power of the soft candle.

Another aspect of inertia is that objects tend to remain at rest if they are not moving. For this reason it is possible to knock out the bottom checker in a stack of checkers without disturbing the rest of the stack.

How to Perform Magic with Checkers

MATERIALS	ten or more checkers wooden ruler
KEY TERMS	Inertia: The tendency of all objects and matter in the universe to remain still, or, if moving, to go on moving in the same direction unless acted upon by some outside force.
	Velocity: Quickness of motion; the rate of motion, speed.
WHAT WILL BE DISCOVERED	Because of the inertia of the stack of checkers, the checkers will remain stacked even when the bottom checker in the stack is knocked away.

Stack about ten checkers on top of a desk or table. Sharply strike the bottom checker with the wooden ruler. It should be possible to knock the checker you strike out of the stack without disturbing the rest of the stack, which is held in place by the inertia of the stack.

Immovable Quarter

Why is it hard to push a car when it is stopped or to stop it when it is moving? Because of inertia. Perhaps you've also noticed that it seems to take more force (either pulling or pushing) to start and stop a moving object than to keep it moving.

You can demonstrate the principle of inertia by duplicating a very simple experiment that appeared in *Scientific American* in 1887. Because of inertia, you will be able to remove a card from under a coin, without touching the coin.

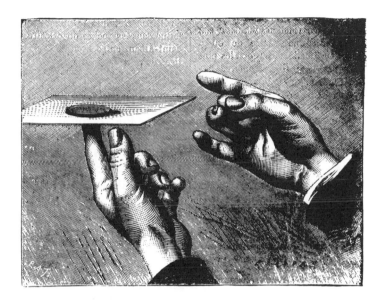

How to Demonstrate the Principle of Inertia

MATERIALS	one quarter one playing card or 3″ × 5″ index card
KEY TERMS	Inertia: The tendency of all objects and matter in the universe to remain still, or, if moving, to go on moving in the same direction unless acted upon by some outside force.
WHAT WILL BE DISCOVERED	Because of inertia, the quarter will remain at rest on your fingertip even when the card is flicked out from under it.

Balance the card on one of your index fingers. Place the quarter on top of the card, just above your index finger, as shown in the illustration above.

Quickly flick the edge of the card with your index finger as shown in the illustration. If you have flicked the card in a horizontal direction, it should fly out from under the quarter, leaving the coin at rest on your fingertip. (Hint: Weights of coins have changed since the nineteenth century. You will find the experiment easier to perform successfully if you flick the *long* edge of the card. You might also try the experiment with a half-dollar or a smaller card, like a business card.)

Spinning Marble

Another interesting aspect of the principle of inertia is that it causes a moving object to keep moving at a constant speed. Inertia also causes the object to move in a straight line. A consequence of this is that if the object is moving against an inwardly curved vertical surface, it will cling to the surface—because of centrifugal force.

You can easily demonstrate this concept, which may be difficult to understand at first, by adapting an experiment that was reported in a *Scientific American Supplement* in 1882. In the magazine experiment a penny and lampshade were used. You can demonstrate the same principle using a soda bottle and a marble.

How to Demonstrate the Force of Inertia

MATERIALS quart soda bottle
marble

KEY TERMS Inertia: The tendency of all objects and matter in the universe to remain still, or, if moving, to go on moving in the same direction unless acted upon by some outside force.

Centrifugal force: The aspect of inertia that causes a body moving around a center to move away from the center.

WHAT WILL BE That the centrifugal force generated by the rotary
DISCOVERED motion of your hands moving the bottle will keep the marble rolling around the inside of the bottle, and the force of inertia will keep the marble from immediately falling to the bottom.

Place the marble in the soda bottle. Start it rolling around the inside of the bottle. Holding the bottle with your hands, start moving it with a slight circular motion.

As you move the bottle faster, if you lower it slightly, the marble will climb up the side of the bottle. As you slow down the circular motion of the bottle, the marble will gradually roll toward the bottom of the bottle.

55

7.
Sound

Ringing Spoon

An interesting experiment from the nineteenth century demonstrating the conduction of sounds through solids involved attaching the center of a four-foot length of string to a spoon. When the ends of the string were put up to one's ears and the spoon was allowed to swing against the end of a table, a loud, bell-like sound was heard through the ends of the string.

How to Make a Spoon Ring

MATERIALS   4' length of string or thin wire
             teaspoon

KEY TERMS   Sound: What is or can be heard: sensation pro-
             duced in the organs of hearing by vibrations
             transmitted through gases, solids or liquids.

             Vibration: Rapid movement to and fro; quivering
             movement.

WHAT WILL BE   Because spoons are curved, like bells, they can
DISCOVERED   vibrate to produce sounds that can be amplified by
               conducting them directly to your ears through
               string or wire. All sounds are created by vibration.

In order to get a ringing sound from the spoon, tie the string around it so that the spoon balances from the middle of the length of string as shown in the illustration.

Gently place the ends of the string in your ears. Let the spoon swing against the edge of a table. A bell-like sound should result. Different sizes of spoons will sound different. Larger spoons will make lower-pitched sounds, smaller spoons higher-pitched sounds.

Using a piece of wire instead of a piece of string to conduct the sound generated from the spoon will give you an even clearer sound.

NOTE: *If you use a piece of wire instead of string as your conductor, be particularly careful not to hurt yourself when you place the wires to your ears!*

String Telephone

Long before the electric telephone was invented by the American inventor Alexander Graham Bell (1847–1922) scientists knew that sound could be transmitted through different types of solid objects. A simple string telephone that was popular with children during the nineteenth century demonstrates this principle extremely well.

Two short mouthpieces (made from tin cans) were each covered with a piece of thin oiled paper stretched tightly to form a diaphragm. The two diaphragms, which served as both transmitters and receivers, were connected by a long piece of string. When the string was stretched tight a conversation could be carried on between

the two telephones. When one person talked into his or her mouthpiece, the sound waves caused the diaphragm to vibrate, and the vibrations were then transmitted over the string to the other diaphragm, which served as a receiver.

How to Make a String Telephone

MATERIALS   two large, empty soft-drink or milkshake paper cups
scissors
heavy thread that won't stretch
two pieces of a round, wooden toothpick, each ½″ long
a needle with a very large eye

KEY TERMS   Diaphragm: A thin disk that vibrates rapidly when receiving or producing sounds. Used in telephones, microphones, loudspeakers and other instruments.

Telephone: An apparatus or system for sending sound or speech over wires using electrical impulses.

Vibration: Rapid movement to and fro; quivering movement.

WHAT WILL BE DISCOVERED Sound can be transmitted best through solid objects. A vibrating string can transmit sound. When the vibration is stopped, the sound will stop.

Cut a twenty-five-foot length of heavy thread. Thread the needle with this. Very carefully pierce the center of the bottom of one of the paper cups as illustrated. The bottoms of the cups will serve as diaphragms for your telephones. Remove the needle from the thread. Knot the end of the thread around a piece of toothpick on the inside of the cup. This device will prevent the thread from pulling out of the diaphragm. Repeat this step for the other paper cup with the other end of the thread.

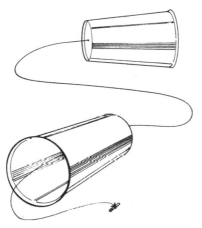

In order to use your paper-cup telephone two people will have to pick up the paper cups and carefully walk away from each other until the line is stretched tight. Do not let the line touch anything else. If it does, the vibrations traveling over the line will be interfered with. Be careful not to pull the line so tight that it pulls loose from the diaphragms.

When one person speaks into a cup, the sound waves will cause a vibration in the diaphragm of that cup (the transmitter) which will be transmitted through the line to the other diaphragm (the receiver). The person holding the cup that is the receiver should be able to hear what is being said into the transmitter at the other end. In order to make listening over the line easier and clearer, hold the receiver directly against one ear and cover your other ear with your other hand.

Glass Harmonica

The glass harmonica (more properly "armonica") is an extremely interesting and beautiful musical instrument invented in 1761 by the famous American scientist and statesman Benjamin Franklin (1706–1790). Although almost totally unknown today, it was once popular enough for the great Austrian composer Wolfgang Amadeus Mozart (1756–1791) to have written a quintet for the glass harmonica, flute, oboe, viola and violoncello (1791).

Franklin's harmonica consisted of a series of overlapping bowl-shaped glasses arranged, on their side, on a spindle. When the spindle was turned around, the rims of the glasses were moistened as they passed through a container of water below. Music was made on the glass harmonica by rubbing the wet glass rims with a ringer. A simple version of the glass harmonica which you can easily make is illustrated below.

How to Make a Glass Harmonica

MATERIALS   eight identical glasses (these should be as light in weight as possible)
pitcher full of water

sponge to clean up spilled water
bottle of food coloring

KEY TERMS   Sound: What is or can be heard; sensation produced in the organs of hearing by vibrations
transmitted by the air or some other medium.

WHAT WILL BE   A different amount of water in each glass will leave
DISCOVERED   a different column of air in each glass. The sound
produced by rubbing your hand over the rim of
each glass will vary according to the height of the
column of air in each glass.

A simple but very effective glass harmonica can be made by lining
up eight identical glasses in a row. Fill each of the glasses with a little
bit of water. The first glass should have only a little bit of water in it,
the next a little more, and so on. The last should be almost filled to
the top.

Wet your index finger and run it over the rim of each of the
glasses. With a little bit of practice you should be able to get sounds
from the glasses. Each will sound different according to how much
water it has in it. The tone depends on the length of the column of air
in the glass.

You might find it fun to take a pitch pipe and tune the glasses to
certain specific notes by pouring water in and out of them. Pour a
small amount of food coloring into one of the glasses filled with
water. When you rub your finger along the edge of the glass you
should actually be able to see the sound waves you are creating
vibrating across the water's surface.

Dancing Wire

An interesting experiment that was included in many nineteenth-century science books was based on the principle of the glass harmonica. A wire was placed across the top of a glass filled with water. A second glass was filled with exactly the same amount of water. When the rim of the second glass was rubbed with a moist finger, the piece of metal on the first glass would vibrate and dance in response to the sound being generated. This phenomenon is known as resonance. In other words, the vibration in one object will set up a similar vibration in a second object, strongest when the objects are identical.

How to Make a Piece of Wire Dance on the Rim of a Glass

MATERIALS
: two identical glasses, as light in weight as possible
  pitcher of water
  sponge
  one thin piece of wire, ½″ longer than the diameter of the glasses

KEY TERMS
: Resonance: A reinforcing and prolonging of sound by reflection or by vibration of other objects. Identical objects most readily pick up each other's vibrations.

Sound: What is or can be heard; sensation produced in the organs of hearing by vibrations transmitted by the air or some other medium.

WHAT WILL BE DISCOVERED The sound waves in the second glass will travel through the air to the first glass, setting off a vibration in the water that will cause the piece of wire to vibrate and dance along the rim of the glass.

Pour equal amounts of water into each glass. Bend down the edges of the wire so that there is a quarter of an inch on either side as shown in the illustration above. Place the wire across the top of the glass.

Gently rub the rim of the other glass with the tip of your finger. The piece of wire should begin to vibrate along the rim of the first glass in response to the sound waves you are creating.

A Simple Phonograph

The American inventor Thomas Alva Edison (1847–1931) is known for a number of important discoveries including the first practical light bulb. He also invented the phonograph in 1877.

Edison's phonograph consisted of a rotating cylinder with a groove cut into its surface. A sheet of tinfoil was wrapped around the cylinder. As the cylinder revolved it moved between two small horns

that were fixed in place. One of these horns served as a mouthpiece and included a diaphragm with a small metal stylus attached to it; the point of the stylus rested on the tin cylinder. When someone spoke into the mouthpiece and the cylinder rotated, the vibrations of the diaphragm were recorded on the sheet of tinfoil by the stylus. These vibrations were reproduced by a second stylus with a rounded head.

How to Make a Simple Phonograph

| MATERIALS | empty soft-drink or milkshake paper cup |
| | straight pin |

KEY TERMS   Phonograph: An instrument that reproduces sounds from phonograph records.

Sound: What is or can be heard; sensation produced in the organs of hearing by vibrations transmitted through gases, solids or liquids.

WHAT WILL BE   That sound can be recorded and reproduced
DISCOVERED   through the use of simple devices, such as a stylus and a diaphragm.

Insert the straight pin through the cup as illustrated below. Make sure that the tip of the pin extends slightly beyond the bottom of the cup.

Find a very old record that you do not mind having damaged. Place it on a record player at the proper speed. Leave the tone arm on the side of the record player. Holding in your hand the speaker you have made, place the pin in the groove. The pin will vibrate as it moves across the grooves in the record, transferring the vibrations to the diaphragm and making sounds.

8
Gravity

Uphill-Rolling Object

Sometimes demonstrations of scientific principles seem to contradict what you have learned about science. For example, you would assume that the force of gravity would cause a pair of conical objects, such as two funnels joined together, placed on a slope, to roll downhill. However, as the experiment illustrated below demonstrates, the funnels, or a pair of cones, can actually be made to appear to roll uphill.

How to Cause a Double Cone to Roll Uphill

MATERIALS   two funnels, the same size
              masking tape
              large book
              small book
              two dowels or sticks

KEY TERMS   Center of gravity: The point in a body around
              which its weight is evenly balanced.

              Gravity: The natural force that causes objects to
              move or tend to move toward the center of the
              earth.

WHAT WILL BE Even though the funnels appear to be rolling
DISCOVERED   upward, their center of gravity is actually moving
              downhill, because the two sticks are spread apart,
              allowing the center of gravity to sink lower and
              lower.

Tape the rims of the funnels together. If you can't find two equal-sized funnels, you can make them out of cardboard.

Stand the large book on its side and the small book on its side on a table or desk as shown in the illustration above. Place the two dowels or sticks across the spines of the books as illustrated. On the spine of the large book, the two dowels must be farther apart than they are on the spine of the smaller book.

When you place the double cone at the bottom of the slope formed by the sticks, it will actually begin to roll uphill!

Mixing a Liquid Parfait

Have you ever noticed a patch of motor oil on the surface of a puddle of water? The oil is able to remain on the surface because it is lighter than the water.

The principle that different liquids have different weights or densities also makes it possible for different layers of liquids to be added to the same glass and yet remain separated from each other. You can mix up your own liquid parfait to demonstrate some science magic in a tall, cone-shaped glass like the one illustrated below from an old science book.

How to Mix Your Own Liquid Parfait

MATERIALS   parfait or cone-shaped glass (if you do not have a parfait glass you can use any tall, slender glass)
ice-cold coffee, sweetened with sugar
water
vegetable oil
meat or turkey baster

KEY TERMS   Density: The quantity of matter in a unit of volume or area.

Weight: How heavy a thing is.

WHAT WILL BE DISCOVERED   Because different liquids have different densities they will remain in separate layers even when placed together in the same glass.

Pour a layer of coffee, about one inch deep, into the glass. Fill the baster with approximately the same amount of water. Carefully place the baster inside the glass so that the tip is just above the coffee. Squeeze the baster so that the water slowly dribbles out of the tip. Since the water is lighter than the sweetened coffee, it should form the second layer of the parfait by resting on top of the coffee.

67

Wash out the baster and then fill it with vegetable oil and repeat the same process. Because the vegetable oil is lighter than the water, it will rest on top of the water, forming the third level of the parfait.

You can use the baster to experiment with many different liquids to discover which ones are heavier and which ones are lighter.

Acrobatic Coin

The force of gravity makes some wonderful scientific tricks possible. Imagine being able to make a coin rest on its edge on the rim of a glass! As you can see in the illustration of the demonstration, two forks are used to help establish the equilibrium of the coin on the rim of the glass.

How to Balance a Coin on the Rim of a Glass

MATERIALS	quarter
	two forks
	glass
KEY TERMS	Equilibrium: Balance.

Gravity: The natural force that causes objects to move or tend to move toward the center of the earth.

Center of gravity: The point in a body around which its weight is evenly balanced.

Tangent: In contact, touching; touching a curve or surface at one point but not intersecting.

WHAT WILL BE DISCOVERED — Once the coin is balanced at any point on an imaginary vertical line running through its center of gravity, it will remain balanced on its edge on the rim of the glass.

Insert the quarter between the prongs of the two forks. Hold a fork in each hand and place the edge of the coin flat on the rim of the glass. Keep adjusting the position of the coin and forks by shifting the forks until they balance as shown above.

When the equilibrium of the forks and coin is established, the center of gravity of the combined forks and coin will be on the circumference formed by the rim of the glass. The balance depends both on the weight of the forks on both sides of the coin and on their distance from the center of gravity. A circus tightrope walker often uses a long stick in the same way as the forks are used in this demonstration for balancing.

The demonstration can be even more dramatic. Fill the glass with water. You should actually be able to pour water from the glass, with the forks and coin balanced on its rim, into another glass without causing the coin to fall off the rim of the glass.

Domino Acrobatics

Dominoes were invented in China at least three hundred years ago. Originally, domino pieces were used for telling fortunes. By the mid-1700's Europeans were using them to gamble and to play different types of games.

Dominoes are also used to build fantastically long constructions that can be completely knocked over by pushing over the first domino in the line, thus setting off a chain reaction. Domino pieces can be used to demonstrate other tricks, such as the one illustrated below, in which a complete set of dominoes (twenty-eight pieces) is supported by a single piece.

How to Demonstrate Domino Acrobatics

MATERIALS
set of dominoes

KEY TERMS
Gravity: The natural force that causes objects to move or tend to move toward the center of the earth.

Center of gravity: The point in a body around which its weight is evenly balanced.

Equilibrium: Balance.

WHAT WILL BE DISCOVERED
Because the center of gravity of the complete domino construction passes through the single supporting bottom piece, the entire structure will be balanced and won't fall over.

Begin the structure illustrated on the previous page with four dominoes placed as shown below.

Continue adding dominoes so that you are duplicating the structure in the first illustration. After the structure is almost complete, carefully remove the two outside bottom dominoes and place them on the top to complete the structure. It should stand, supported by the single domino, because the center of gravity of the construction passes through the single supporting domino, providing equilibrium for the whole structure.

9.
Topology

Slipping Through an Index Card

Imagine holding up a three-by-five-inch index card in front of your friends and telling them that you will slip it over your head and pull it down to your feet! They will take one look at the card and exclaim, "No way!"

How to Slip Through a Three-by-Five-Inch Index Card

MATERIALS	one 3″ × 5″ index card scissors
KEY TERMS	Topology: The study of surfaces and the mapping of them. The way a surface is analyzed and taken apart determines to a large extent how we understand it.
WHAT WILL BE DISCOVERED	That the principles of the topology of a surface area make it possible to alter the surface area of a 3″ × 5″ index card.

Fold the index card in half, lengthwise. Cut a slit along the fold that doesn't quite reach either end of the card, as shown in part 1 of the illustration (the card used there is a playing card).

Fold the card again along the same crease. Carefully cut slits at right angles to the first cut along the centerfold. Make the first cut from the top, or the centerfold. Then alternate with a cut from the outside edge of the card. Continue making cuts across the card, alternating from the top to bottom as shown in part 2 of the illustration.

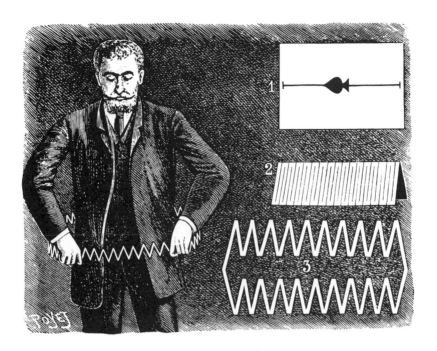

Gently stretch the card open by pulling on the two ends as shown in part 3 of the illustration. You should end up with a thin zigzag circle of paper that is large enough to slip over your head and down your body to your feet.

10.
Light

Burning Lenses and Mirrors

According to legend, the ancient Greek scientist Archimedes (287?–212 B.C.) destroyed a fleet of Roman ships by using "burning mirrors" to set the ships' sails on fire. The legend might very well be true, as you will discover when you experiment with burning lenses and mirrors.

A simple trick from the nineteenth century involved setting a piece of thread in a sealed glass bottle on fire by focusing light on it with a magnifying glass. You can see this being done in the illustration below.

How to Make a Burning Lens or Mirror

MATERIALS
magnifying glass
magnifying mirror, such as a shaving mirror or a makeup mirror
sheet of dull black paper

KEY TERMS
Magnify: To cause the size of an object to appear larger than it really is.

Lens: A curved piece of glass or other transparent material that brings closer together or sends wider apart the rays of light passing through it.

Magnifying glass: A lens or combination of lenses that causes things to look larger than they really are.

WHAT WILL BE DISCOVERED
Because all the rays of light coming through a magnifying glass are directed onto a very small point, the energy contained in the rays will be concentrated and will generate enough heat to set on fire a piece of paper placed precisely at that point.

NOTE: *When conducting this experiment using a magnifying glass or a mirror, do not focus the light rays on any part of your body. If you do, you could seriously burn yourself! Also, be careful not to set anything on fire except the piece of paper.*

To be successful, this experiment needs to be conducted on a bright, sunny day. Take a magnifying glass and focus the light from it onto a piece of black paper. Move the paper back and forth until you get the smallest point of light possible focused on the paper. If you

hold your hand steady you should be able to concentrate enough light to set the paper on fire.

You can focus the light of the sun in the same way using a shaving or makeup mirror instead of a magnifying glass. The curved surface of the mirror will collect light and focus it on one point of the paper. If you hold the mirror in place long enough, and the sun is bright enough, the concentrated light rays will ignite the paper.

Concave mirrors reflecting sunlight are used to generate steam power and electricity. At Odeillo in southern France a large mirror focusing sunlight boils water for a steam-turbine electrical generator at temperatures of over three thousand degrees Celsius.

11.

Geometry

Drawing an Ellipse

An ellipse is a curved figure shaped like an oval with both ends alike. It has two focal points. A peculiar characteristic of the ellipse is that the sum of the distance between any point on the ellipse and one focal point and the distance between the same point and the other focal point is always the same number.

Normally the construction of an ellipse is an extremely difficult process involving the use of specialized patterns or complicated geometric formulas. However, during the 1800's, carpenters and bricklayers used a very simple method for constructing partial elliptical arches.

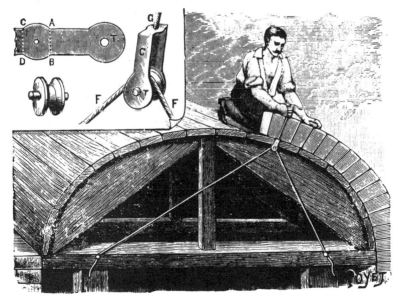

They attached a long piece of rope to two different points on a beam running underneath the soon-to-be-built arch. This beam formed the major axis of the ellipse. The two different points where the rope was attached to the beam were the focal points of the ellipse. The rope ran through a pulley that could be lifted to keep the rope taut. The illustration shows that as the pulley was lifted and moved from right to left, it followed the curve of the partial ellipse.

How to Draw an Ellipse

MATERIALS	two thumbtacks or pushpins sheet of heavy cardboard 18" piece of string pencil ruler
KEY TERMS	Ellipse: A geometrical figure shaped like an oval with both ends alike. Pulley: A wheel with a grooved rim in which a rope can run and so change the direction of a pull. This simple machine can be used to lift weights.
WHAT WILL BE DISCOVERED	How to construct a simple ellipse without the use of mathematical formulas.

Tie the ends of the piece of string together. Stick the thumbtacks into the piece of cardboard about six inches apart. The thumbtacks from the focal points of the ellipse. Be sure that the thumbtacks are pushed in enough so that they won't pull out. Place the loop of string around the tacks.

Put the pencil on the inside of the loop of string and pull the string taut. Make a mark with the pencil at the point where the string is pulled taut. Continue to move the point of the pencil around the tacks, keeping the string pulled taut, and continuing the pencil mark through each successive point.

As you move the string and pencil around the tacks, you will be drawing a perfect ellipse. The apparatus you have constructed obeys the mathematical definition of an ellipse. If you add the distance between any point on the ellipse (where the pencil is) and one thumbtack to the distance between the same point and the other thumbtack, you will always get the same number.

Experiment with placing the tacks closer together (to make a rounder ellipse) or farther apart (to make a longer, narrower ellipse).

12.
Mechanics

Straw Lever

Imagine being able to lift a decanter or glass bottle with a broom straw! As the illustration below from an 1880 *Scientific American Supplement* shows, it is possible to do just that.

How to Lift a Glass Bottle with a Straw

MATERIALS
: glass beer bottle or water bottle
  stiff straw, reed or long broom straw

KEY TERMS
: Lever: A simple machine consisting of a bar that turns on a fixed support called a fulcrum and is used to transmit effort and motion.

WHAT WILL BE DISCOVERED
: The bent straw inside the bottle will act as a lever which you can use to lift up the bottle. The fixed support or fulcrum of the lever is at the point where the straw is bent. The section of the straw between the fulcrum and the inside top of the bottle is the load arm. The other section of the straw, between the fulcrum and the lifting force, is the effort arm of the lever.

Bend the straw so that it forms a sharp angle. The shorter piece of the straw should be almost as long as the cylindrical part of the bottle. The other part of the straw must be long enough to extend outside of the bottle when inserted into it.

Hold the two parts of the straw together as you push them through the mouth of the bottle. The tip of the shorter piece of straw should wedge itself against the inside top of the cylindrical part of the bottle.

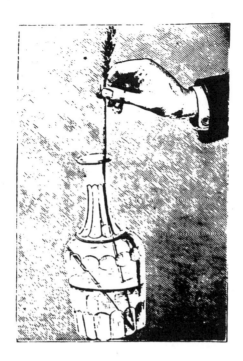

Grab the tip of the longer piece of straw and pull up. If the straw is positioned correctly inside the bottle, it should act as a lever and allow you to use it to lift up the bottle.

13.
Heat

Hot-Air Detector

The fact that hot air rises has been known for thousands of years. In fact, hot air is a gas. The hotter it gets, the faster the particles that make up the gas move. It is hot air rising that distorts the light and causes things to look wavy when you are driving down a road on a warm day. It is also hot air that makes it possible for one kind of passenger-carrying balloon to float through the sky.

In ancient Greece, simple devices were made that would move when brought in contact with rising currents of hot air. Similar devices were popular as toys for children during the nineteenth century.

How to Make a Hot-Air Detector

MATERIALS
one piece of paper
scissors
pencil or pen
needle and thread

KEY TERMS
Air: The mixture of gases that surrounds the earth.

Gas: Any substance that is neither solid nor liquid and that has no shape or size of its own and can expand without limit.

WHAT WILL BE
DISCOVERED
The heat of the light bulb turned on will cause the particles that make up the air (a gas) above the light bulb to rise and move more rapidly, setting the spiral spinning.

Photocopy or trace the pattern illustrated below. Cut out the pattern you have transferred to the piece of paper in order to make a spiral. Knot the end of the thread and string it through the top of the spiral so that it hangs easily by the thread.

Suspend the spiral above an electric light bulb. Turn on the light bulb. The hot-air currents generated by the light bulb will set the spiral slowly spinning.

HOT-AIR DETECTOR PATTERN

14.
Chemical Absorption

Moisture-detecting Mermaid

One of the most popular inexpensive toys during the late 1800's was the "sensitive mermaid." In fact, the toy was a simple moisture detector. Made from gelatinized paper, it would absorb perspiration (primarily water and salt) when held in the palm of a hand. Since the moisture did not penetrate through the gelatinized paper, one side of the mermaid was wet while the other side remained dry. This would cause the mermaid to curl up and move back and forth in a twisting motion.

How to Make a Moisture-detecting Mermaid

MATERIALS   scissors
small piece of cellophane (not plastic food wrap)
pencil

| KEY TERMS | Moisture: Water or other liquid suspended in very small drops in the air or spread on a surface. |
| WHAT WILL BE DISCOVERED | That certain materials, such as gelatinized paper, cellophane and human hair, expand when they become moist and then shrink when they dry. |

Trace the pattern of the mermaid onto the piece of cellophane. Cut it out.

MOISTURE-DETECTING MERMAID PATTERN

Place the mermaid in the palm of your hand and watch it move back and forth. The side touching your palm absorbs the perspiration, causing it to expand. Since the other side remains dry and does not expand, the mermaid will curl upward. Moisture-detecting materials are used in such scientific instruments as hygrometers.

Sources of
Historical Illustrations

Titles in quotation marks are of sections in this book, according to the order of which the following list is organized.

"How Many Quarters Will a Glass Full of Water Hold?" Gaston Tissandier, *Les Récréations Scientifiques* (Paris: G. Masson Editeur, 1881), p. 4.

"Floating Needle." Tom Tit [Arthur Good], *La Science Amusante, Première Série; 100 Nouvelles Expériences* (Paris: Librairie Larousse, 1890), n.p.

"Snuffing a Candle with a Soap Bubble." Tom Tit [Arthur Good], *La Science Amusante, Deuxième Série; 100 Nouvelles Expériences* (Paris: Librairie Larousse, 1892), p. 143.

"Motorized Paper Fish." Tom Tit [Arthur Good], *La Science Amusante, Première Série; 100 Nouvelles Expériences* (Paris: Librairie Larousse, 1890), n.p.

"Perpetual Dancers." Tom Tit [Arthur Good], *La Science Amusante, Troisième Série; 100 Nouvelles Expériences* (Paris: Librairie Larousse, [1894?]), p. 37.

"Air 'Boils' Water." Tom Tit [Arthur Good], *La Science Amusante, Troisième Série; 100 Nouvelles Expériences* (Paris: Librairie Larousse, [1894?]), p. 23.

"Air Holds Up Water." Gaston Tissandier, *Les Récréations Scientifiques* (Paris: G. Masson Editeur, 1881), p. 34.

"Magdeburg Sphere." *Scientific American Supplement* 618 (November 5, 1887), p. 9877.

"Simple Diving Bell." Gaston Tissandier, *Popular Scientific Recreations* [trans. Henry Frith] (New York: Ward, Lock, and Co., [1890?]), title page.

"Cartesian Diver." Gaston Tissandier, *Les Récréations Scientifiques* (Paris: G. Masson Editeur, 1881), p. 334.

"Soap-Bubble Passenger." *Scientific American Supplement* 608 (August 27, 1887), p. 9716.

"Suspended Pea." *Scientific American,* May 28, 1887, p. 342.

"Blowing an Egg Out of a Cup." *Scientific American Supplement* 243 (August 28, 1880), p. 1.

"Air Glue." *Scientific American Supplement* 279 (May 7, 1881), p. 4448.

"3-D Vision." Tom Tit [Arthur Good], *La Science Amusante, Deuxième Série; 100 Nouvelles Expériences* (Paris: Librairie Larousse, 1892), p. 135.

"Thaumatrope." Gaston Tissandier, *Les Récréations Scientifiques* (Paris: G. Masson Editeur, 1881), p. iii.

"Moving-Picture Machine." *Scientific American,* November 26, 1881, p. 338.

"Distorted Picture." *The Boy's Own Book,* 7th ed. (London: Vizetelly, Branston and Co., 1831), n.p.

"Color Tops." J. C. Maxwell, *Scientific Papers of James Clerk Maxwell,* ed. by W. P. Niven (Cambridge: Cambridge University Press, 1890), part I, p. 127.

"Newton's Rings." Tom Tit [Arthur Good], *La Science Amusante, Troisième Série; 100 Nouvelles Expériences* (Paris: Librairie Larousse, [1894?]), p. 133.

"Distorted Images." *Scientific American Supplement* (May 7, 1881), p. 4448.

"Detecting Static Electrical Charges." Tom Tit [Arthur Good], *La Science Amusante, Deuxième Série; 100 Nouvelles Expériences* (Paris: Librairie Larousse, 1892), p. 113.

"Electrified Dice." Tom Tit [Arthur Good], *La Science Amusante, Troisième Série; 100 Nouvelles Expériences* (Paris: Librairie Larousse, [1894?]), p. 95.

"Dancing Soap Bubbles." Tom Tit [Arthur Good], *La Science Amusante, Troisième Série; 100 Nouvelles Expériences* (Paris: Librairie Larousse, [1894?]), p. 131.

"Floating Magnets." *Scientific American,* February 12, 1887, p. 105.

"Water That Won't Spill." Tom Tit [Arthur Good], *La Science Amusante, Première Série; 100 Nouvelles Expériences* (Paris: Librairie Larousse, 1890), p. 151.

"Magic with Coins." *Scientific American Supplement* 608 (August 27, 1887), p. 9716.

"More Magic with Coins." *Scientific American Supplement* 608 (August 27, 1887), p. 9716.

"Elevated Napkin Ring." *Scientific American Supplement* 279 (May 7, 1881), p. 4448.

"Magic with Checkers." *Scientific American Supplement* 247 (September 25, 1880), p. 3930.

"Immovable Quarter." *Scientific American,* March 26, 1887, p. 201.

"Spinning Marble." *Scientific American Supplement* 321 (February 25, 1882), p. 5122.

"Ringing Spoon." *Scientific American Supplement* 232 (June 12, 1880), title page.

"String Telephone." *Scientific American,* February 19, 1887, p. 121.

"Glass Harmonica." *Scientific American Supplement* 266 (February 5, 1881), p. 4238.

"Dancing Wire." Tom Tit [Arthur Good], *La Science Amusante, Troisième Série; 100 Nouvelles Expériences* (Paris: Librairie Larousse, [1894?]), p. 91.

"A Simple Phonograph." *Scientific American,* July 6, 1878, p. 5.

"Uphill-Rolling Object." Tom Tit [Arthur Good], *La Science Amusante, Deuxième Série; 100 Nouvelles Expériences* (Paris: Librairie Larousse, 1892), p. 15.

"Mixing a Liquid Parfait." Tom Tit [Arthur Good], *La Science Amusante, Deuxième Série; 100 Nouvelles Expériences* (Paris: Librairie Larousse, 1892), p. 19.

"Acrobatic Coin." *Scientific American Supplement* 618 (November 5, 1887), p. 9877.

"Domino Acrobatics." *Scientific American Supplement* 297 (September 10, 1881), n.p.

"Slipping Through an Index Card." Tom Tit [Arthur Good], *La Science Amusante, Première Série; 100 Nouvelles Expériences* (Paris: Librairie Larousse, 1890), p. 223.

"Burning Lenses and Mirrors." Tom Tit [Arthur Good], *La Science Amusante, Deuxième Série; 100 Nouvelles Expériences* (Paris: Librairie Larousse, 1892), p. 129.

"Drawing an Ellipse." Tom Tit [Arthur Good], *La Science Amusante, Troisième Série; 100 Nouvelles Expériences* (Paris: Librairie Larousse, [1894?]), p. 157.

"Straw Lever." *Scientific American Supplement* 247 (September 25, 1880), p. 3930.

"Hot-Air Detector." *Scientific American Supplement* 279 (May 7, 1881), p. 4448.

"Moisture-detecting Mermaid." *Scientific American,* January 22, 1887, p. 56.